D1567581

INDIANAPOLIS MEMORIES

Festivals Cookbook

INDIANAPOLIS MEMORIES

Festivals Cookbook

Edited by Ginny Berg
Artwork by K. P. Singh

Memories Press
Indianapolis, Indiana
1997

First Edition

Text © 1997 by Ginny Berg
Artwork © 1997 by K. P. Singh

ISBN 0-89730-231-1

Printed in Canada

Memories Press is a publishing imprint
of R. J. Berg & Company, Publishers.

Memories Press
P. O. Box 30225
Indianapolis, IN 46230-0225
(800) 638-3909

A man hath no better thing under the sun,
than to eat, and to drink, and to be merry.

Ecclesiastes 8:15

Contents

Illustrations

Acknowledgments

500 Festival: Diana Brobst, 500 Festival Associates, Inc.; Jug Eckert, Jug's Catering

Applefest: Cristy Sagalowsky; Lisa A. Hendrickson, Park Tudor School

Balkan Festival: Ann Foreman

Festival of Gingerbread: Julie Saetre, Conner Prairie

Fiesta: Rolando Quintana, Executive Administrator, and the Fiesta Board of Directors

Greek Festival: Irene M. Sarris

Indiana Black Expo's Summer Celebration: Twyler Jenkins, Charlotte Brown, Donna L. Hayes

Indianapolis Convention & Visitors Association: Mary K. Huggard

International Festival: Chao-Hung Lee, Betty Bunnell, Alice Davis, Carson C. St. John, K. P. and Janice Singh

Italian Street Festival: Marie Pittman-Oechsle, David Page, Maggie Minardo Greene, Bernie Greene

Midsummer Fest: Todd Watson, Cathedral Arts; Sandi Fowler, Fowler Catering

Oktoberfest: German-American Cultural Center

Penrod Arts Fair: Bernie Jones

Strawberry Festival: Florida Strawberry Growers Association

Western Festival: Amy Rubin, Eiteljorg Museum of American Indians and Western Art; Brad Bayliff, Steve Daily, Mike Carter

Introduction

Festivals are for fun!

Festivals are for families and friends.

And ethnic festivals are an opportunity for participants to renew pride in their heritage and cement their relationship with the community.

—Marge Hanley
The Indianapolis News
October 20, 1982

There is no better description of what festivals are all about.

Indianapolis Memories: Festivals Cookbook is a collection of recipes and artwork saluting some of Indianapolis' best-known and most-loved festivals and landmarks. Festivals draw visitors to neighborhoods they might not otherwise explore, and here they encounter new experiences, tastes, and acquaintances.

Those who work long, hard hours to make the festivals possible are motivated by pride of heritage or association. Those who are guests at these festivals are drawn by the enticements of food and festivities. And when the two come together for a few hours, everyone takes away lasting memories of celebration and community.

Indianapolis is not defined by any one of these festivals, but by all of them. Each is as much a part of the whole as the others. We hope you will use *Indianapolis Memories: Festivals Cookbook* as a guidebook for visiting old familiar places and for discovering new ones. It promises to be a journey filled with adventure and fun!

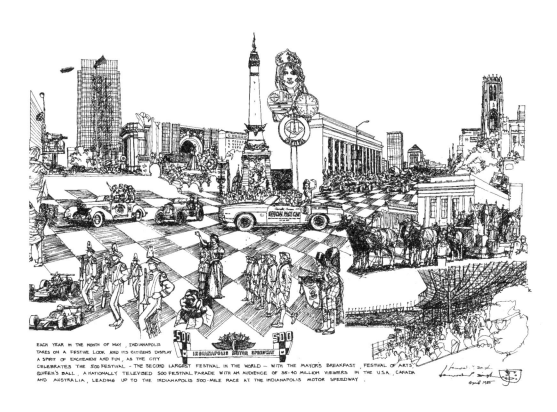

EACH YEAR IN THE MONTH OF MAY, INDIANAPOLIS
TAKES ON A FESTIVE LOOK AND ITS CITIZENS DISPLAY
A SPIRIT OF EXCITEMENT AND FUN, AS THE CITY
CELEBRATES THE 500 FESTIVAL – THE SECOND LARGEST FESTIVAL IN THE WORLD – WITH THE MAYOR'S BREAKFAST, FESTIVAL OF ARTS,
QUEEN'S BALL, A NATIONALLY TELEVISED 500 FESTIVAL PARADE WITH AN AUDIENCE OF 35-40 MILLION VIEWERS IN THE U.S.A., CANADA
AND AUSTRALIA, LEADING UP TO THE INDIANAPOLIS 500-MILE RACE AT THE INDIANAPOLIS MOTOR SPEEDWAY.

500 Festival

Established in 1957 to celebrate the annual running of the 500-Mile Race, the 500 Festival has grown to play a significant part in the life of Indianapolis each spring. May festivities begin with the nation's largest half-marathon and continue until the nation's largest interactive parade has marched through the streets of the city. This recipe is for a treat that has become synonymous with Indy in May—just like those famous words, "Gentlemen, start your engines!"

Fried Biscuits

Vegetable oil for deep-frying
2 packages (10 each) refrigerated biscuits
Apple butter

Pour oil into a deep fryer and heat to 350°F.

Separate biscuits and arrange in a single layer in hot oil. Cook for 90 seconds; turn over carefully and cook 90 seconds on the other side. Remove from oil and drain on paper towels. Repeat process until all biscuits have been cooked. Serve warm with apple butter.

Yield: 8 to 10 servings

Balkan Festival

The Balkan Festival, which began in 1991, was conceived as a way of sharing the Orthodox religion, cultures, and traditions among members of the Balkan community and the citizens of Indianapolis. Three small Orthodox churches on West 16th Street in Indianapolis formed the Balkan Society in 1990, and on the first weekend in June, they present a taste of the cultural heritage of the Balkan region of southwestern Europe.

Sarma
(Stuffed Cabbage Rolls)

1 large head cabbage
3 medium onions, chopped
½ pound bacon, cut into small pieces
½ cup vegetable oil
2 pounds ground beef
1 pound ground pork
4 cloves garlic, finely chopped (divided)
⅔ cup rice

1 tablespoon paprika
Salt and pepper to taste
1 can (27 ounces) sauerkraut, drained
2 pounds smoked pork ribs, smoked shanks or ham
1 can (8 ounces) tomato sauce
1 can (8 ounces) tomato sauce with bits

Remove tough outer leaves and core of cabbage, leaving head intact. Place cabbage in a large pot of boiling water and cook just until leaves can be easily removed (about 10 minutes). Carefully remove leaves, one by one, trying not to tear them. Cut off hard center portion of leaves, keeping each leaf in one piece. Set aside.

Place onions, bacon, and oil in a large pan; sauté until bacon is browned. Add ground beef, ground pork, and half of the garlic; cook until meat is browned. Set aside to cool for 10 minutes.

In a large bowl, combine meat mixture, remaining garlic, rice, paprika, salt, and pepper; mix thoroughly. Place about 2 heaping tablespoons of the meat mixture in the center of a cabbage leaf. Fold sides of cabbage leaf over meat mixture, forming a secure roll. Repeat this procedure until all meat mixture is used.

Put about one-fourth of the sauerkraut in a large pot. Place a layer of cabbage rolls on the sauerkraut. Arrange about one-third of the smoked ribs, shanks or ham on top of the cabbage rolls. Continue alternating layers of sauerkraut, cabbage rolls, and smoked meat, ending with a layer of sauerkraut. Pour both cans of tomato sauce evenly over the top. Add enough water so liquid just covers top layer of sauerkraut, loosening the edges so the liquid reaches all layers. Arrange remaining cabbage leaves over top. Cover pot and simmer for $2^{1}/_{2}$ to 3 hours.

Yield: about 6 servings

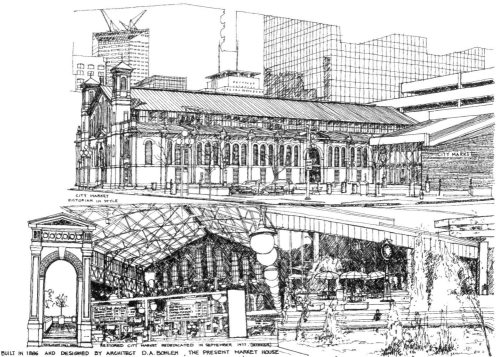

CITY MARKET
VICTORIAN IN STYLE

HARRISON HALL 1888   RESTORED CITY MARKET REDEDICATED IN SEPTEMBER 1977. (INTERIOR)

BUILT IN 1886 AND DESIGNED BY ARCHITECT D.A. BOHLEN, THE PRESENT MARKET HOUSE
STANDS ON THE SITE RESERVED FOR A MARKET IN THE ALEXANDER RALSTON'S PLAN OF 1821 FOR THE "TOWN OF INDIANAPOLIS". THE SIMPLE BRICK EXTER-
IOR PROVIDES AN INTERESTING CONTRAST TO THE INTERIOR OF THE CITY MARKET WITH ITS BEAUTIFULLY DESIGNED FRESH FOOD STALLS, WROUGHT IRON
AND IRON TRUSSES SUPPORTING A RAISED CENTRAL GABLE CLERESTORY ROOF.
OVER THE YEARS, THE MARKET HAS GONE THROUGH MANY CHANGES AND CHALLENGES WHICH IN RECENT YEARS THREATENED ITS VERY SURVIVAL AS A DOWNTOWN
LANDMARK OF DISTINCTION. THE HISTORIC CITY MARKET TODAY IS A CENTER-PIECE OF MARKET SQUARE COMPLEX THANKS TO THE IMAGINATION AND COMMIT-
MENT OF MR. FRANK J. MURRAY (MARKET MASTER 1968-76), HON'BLE RICHARD G. LUGAR (MAYOR 1968-76), STANDHOLDERS AND MARKET PATRONS AND LILLY ENDOWMENT
WHICH PROVIDED $4,751,000 TOWARDS THE MARKET RESTORATION.

Italian Street Festival

On the second weekend in June, the neighborhood around Holy Rosary Church comes alive with the sounds of laughter and music and the aromas of more than 25 different Italian meats, pastas, salads, and desserts. A community favorite since 1984, the Italian Street Festival now attracts as many as 25,000 visitors each year. With entertainment and amusements for all ages, and a colorful Italian Procession followed by Mass in the church, this event nourishes both body and soul.

Antipasto Salad

1 head iceberg lettuce, chopped
Chopped black olives
Chopped green olives
Chopped tomatoes
Ham, cut into bite-size slices

Pepperoni, cut into bite-size slices
Salami, cut into bite-size slices
Pepperoncinis (Italian peppers)
Italian salad dressing
Grated Parmesan cheese

In a large bowl, combine lettuce, black olives, green olives, and tomatoes; toss gently. Add ham, pepperoni, salami, and pepperoncinis. Drizzle with salad dressing and sprinkle with Parmesan cheese. Toss lightly before serving.

Yield: 4 to 6 servings

Note: For ingredients other than lettuce, use about 2 tablespoons of each item per serving, or more or less according to your taste.

Fettuccine Alfredo

1/2 cup salted whipped butter
1 quart (4 cups) whipping cream
8 ounces fontina cheese, grated
8 ounces 100% Parmesan
  cheese, grated
1 tablespoon chopped fresh parsley

Pinch of nutmeg
8 quarts salted water
2 pounds fettuccine
Grated Parmesan cheese
  (for garnish)

Melt butter in a heavy saucepan. Add cream and bring to a boil. Reduce heat and add fontina and Parmesan cheeses; cook, stirring constantly, until cheeses melt and sauce thickens (about 5 minutes). Add parsley and nutmeg. Simmer sauce at very low heat while pasta cooks, stirring often so sauce does not burn.

Bring salted water to a boil. Add fettuccine and cook until pasta is al dente (tender but still firm). Drain, leaving a very small amount of water with the pasta (this will help keep the sauce creamy). Mix pasta and sauce in a large bowl. Sprinkle with extra Parmesan cheese. Serve immediately.

Yield: 10 servings

Italian Cream Cake

Cake

2 cups granulated sugar
½ cup (1 stick) butter
½ cup solid vegetable shortening
1 teaspoon vanilla extract
5 eggs, separated
2 cups flour
1 teaspoon baking soda
½ teaspoon salt
1 cup buttermilk
2 cups shredded or flaked coconut
1 cup chopped pecans

Italian Cream Icing

1 box (16 ounces)
   confectioners' sugar
1 cup chopped pecans
½ cup (1 stick) butter
8 ounces cream cheese
1 teaspoon vanilla extract

Grease three 9-inch cake pans. Preheat oven to 350°F.

To prepare Cake: In a mixing bowl, combine granulated sugar, butter, shortening, and vanilla; beat until creamy. Add egg yolks, one at a time, beating well after each addition. Combine flour, baking soda, and salt. Add dry ingredients and buttermilk to creamed mixture; blend thoroughly. Stir in coconut and pecans. Beat egg whites until stiff peaks form; fold into batter. Spread batter evenly in prepared cake pans. Bake at 350°F for 30 minutes or until a toothpick inserted near the center comes out clean. Remove from oven and cool.

To prepare Italian Cream Icing: In a mixing bowl, combine confectioners' sugar, pecans, butter, cream cheese, and vanilla; beat until smooth. Spread icing between layers and on sides and top of cooled cake.

Yield: 12 to 14 servings

Strawberry Festival

The Strawberry Festival on Monument Circle began in 1965 as a small fund-raising event for Christ Church Episcopal Cathedral. Now this annual June event serves more than six tons of strawberries and as many as 16,000 shortcakes in one day as strawberry lovers feast on "The Works." Family-size portions of this Hoosier classic can be prepared using the simple instructions in the following recipe.

Old-Fashioned Strawberry Shortcake

2½ cups baking mix (such as Bisquick)
½ cup milk
3 tablespoons margarine, melted
4½ tablespoons sugar, divided

¾ cup whipping cream, chilled
2 pints fresh strawberries, sliced and
  sweetened to taste
Vanilla ice cream (if desired)

Preheat oven to 425°F.

In a large mixing bowl, combine baking mix, milk, margarine, and 3 tablespoons sugar; mix until a soft dough forms. Turn out dough onto a cloth lightly dusted with baking mix. Roll dough gently to form a ball; knead eight times. Using a rolling pin, roll out dough to approximately ½-inch thickness. Cut with a 3-inch biscuit cutter. Place biscuits on an ungreased baking sheet. Bake at 425°F for 10 to 12 minutes or until golden brown. Remove from oven and cool.

Beat chilled cream until stiff peaks form, gradually adding remaining 1½ tablespoons sugar while beating. Split biscuits in half and place in serving dishes. Top with strawberries, ice cream, and whipped cream.

Yield: 8 servings

Midsummer Fest

Cathedral Arts' Midsummer Fest on Monument Circle is the largest one-day contemporary music festival in Indianapolis, featuring multiple stages with live music and activities for the entire family. Held since 1976, this event is scheduled every June on the Saturday following the summer solstice. Some of the city's best restaurants and caterers offer up their specialties to the estimated 25,000 people who attend each year. Following is the recipe for one of the event's most popular desserts.

Bananas Foster

¼ cup (½ stick) unsalted butter
¼ cup firmly packed brown sugar
4 ripe bananas, peeled and sliced

¼ teaspoon cinnamon
⅓ cup light or dark rum
Vanilla ice cream

Melt butter in a skillet. Add brown sugar and heat gently, stirring constantly, until sugar melts (about 2 minutes). Add bananas and cook until tender (about 3 to 5 minutes), turning once with a spatula. Sprinkle bananas with cinnamon. Pour rum over bananas and carefully ignite liquor, basting bananas with sauce until the flames subside. Transfer banana slices to four serving dishes. Top each serving of bananas with a scoop of vanilla ice cream. Spoon rum sauce over ice cream. Serve immediately.

Yield: 4 servings

Indiana Black Expo's Summer Celebration

Summer Celebration's activities extend over a full week each July, making it the largest African American cultural event in the nation. More than 500,000 people enjoy the festivities and exhibits, featuring the best in arts, religion, economics, educational and political forums, consumer goods, boxing, and musical entertainment. Indiana Black Expo, Inc., has sponsored the event since it began in 1970. The following recipes are favorites of volunteers who help support this event.

Baked Beans with a Twist

3 cans (16 ounces each) pork and beans
1 can (8 ounces) crushed pineapple,
  drained
1¹/₄ cups firmly packed brown sugar

1 medium onion, chopped
1 small sweet green pepper, chopped
2 slices bacon

Place beans in a large baking dish. Add pineapple, brown sugar, onion, and green pepper; mix well. Place bacon on top of beans. Bake at 325°F for about 1 hour.

Yield: about 6 servings

Note: Ingredients may be mixed in advance and refrigerated several hours or overnight before baking to allow flavors to blend.

Spaghetti Casserole

5 pounds ground beef
1 medium onion, chopped
1 jar (28 ounces) Prego spaghetti sauce
2 cans (14.5 ounces each) chopped
   tomatoes
1 package (16 ounces) spaghetti

Seasonings to taste (basil, bay leaves,
   Italian seasoning, parsley, sugar, salt
   and pepper)
1 package (16 ounces) shredded Cheddar
   cheese
1 package (16 ounces) shredded colby
   cheese

Cook ground beef and onion in a large skillet until meat is browned; drain off any excess fat. Add spaghetti sauce and tomatoes; stir until well blended. Cook spaghetti according to package directions; drain and rinse. Add spaghetti to meat mixture along with seasonings; mix gently. Transfer mixture to a $9\frac{1}{2}$ x14-inch baking pan. Sprinkle cheeses over spaghetti mixture. Bake at 325°F for about 1 hour.

Yield: 6 to 8 servings

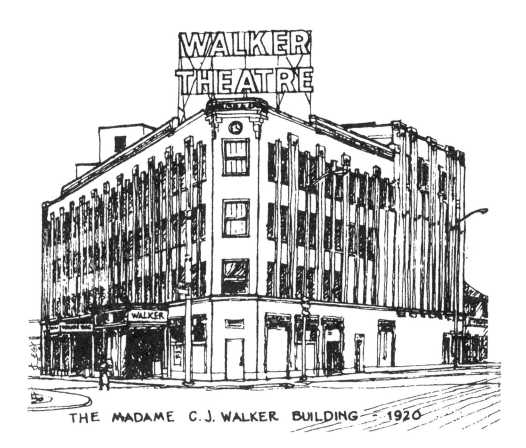

THE MADAME C.J. WALKER BUILDING — 1920

Oktoberfest

The German-American Klub of Indianapolis entertains in the old-world tradition with its Oktoberfest celebration, which spans two weekends in late summer. This event has been held at German Park on the south side of Indianapolis since 1974, and now draws nearly 15,000 visitors each year. The club's motto offers a recipe for the event's success: "Hearty eating and drinking, Dancing with good friends, Makes the heart satisfied and happy all night long."

German Potato Salad

8 potatoes
1/2 pound bacon, cut into small pieces
1/4 cup chopped onion
2 tablespoons flour
3/4 cup (or less) sugar

3/4 cup water
1/2 cup vinegar
6 eggs, hard-boiled and chopped
1 teaspoon salt
1/4 teaspoon pepper

Peel potatoes and cut lengthwise into 1/4-inch slices. Boil for 10 minutes; drain.

Sauté bacon in a skillet; add onion when bacon is almost done. Stir in flour when bacon is browned. Add sugar, water, and vinegar. Cook over medium heat, stirring constantly, until mixture thickens.

In a large bowl, combine potatoes and eggs. Season with salt and pepper. Add bacon dressing and mix gently. Serve warm.

Yield: 6 to 8 servings

Sauerbraten

Marinade

Equal amounts of water and cider
   vinegar (enough to cover meat)
1 onion, sliced
12 whole peppercorns
8 whole cloves
2 tablespoons sugar
1 tablespoon salt
1 bay leaf

Roast and Sauce

1 chuck roast (5 pounds)
3 to 4 tablespoons vegetable oil
10 gingersnaps, crumbled
4 tablespoons browned flour (see note
   below)
1 cup water
Hot cooked noodles

To prepare Marinade: Combine water, vinegar, onion, peppercorns, cloves, sugar, salt, and bay leaf. Place roast in a large glass dish and cover with marinade. Cover and refrigerate for 4 to 5 days.

To prepare Roast and Sauce: When ready to cook roast, drain marinade and reserve. Heat oil in a large, deep skillet. Brown roast on all sides. Add reserved marinade and cook over low heat until meat is fork-tender ($1^1/2$ to 2 hours). Remove meat from skillet and keep warm. Strain sauce, discarding spices; then return strained sauce to skillet. In a small bowl, combine gingersnap crumbs, browned flour, and water. Add to sauce and cook over low heat, stirring constantly, until sauce thickens. Serve slices of roast and sauce over noodles.

Yield: 6 to 8 servings

Note: To brown flour, heat all-purpose flour in a skillet over low heat, stirring constantly, until flour turns a light brown color. Watch carefully so flour does not burn.

Greek Festival

The grounds at Holy Trinity Greek Orthodox Church are transformed into a festive Greek village each September on the first weekend after Labor Day. The Greek Festival made its debut here in 1973, and now more than 15,000 people visit each year to enjoy the full flavor of Greek culture—its food, crafts, music, and dance. Sample a variety of Greek foods (including more than 15 pastries), stroll through the bazaar, and then dance the night away to music played by an authentic Greek band.

Baklava

Pastry

24 ounces walnuts, coarsely ground
$^1/_2$ cup sugar
1 teaspoon cinnamon
$^1/_4$ teaspoon ground cloves
$^1/_4$ teaspoon nutmeg
1 pound sweet (unsalted) butter, melted
1 pound phyllo pastry sheets, thawed

Syrup

4 cups water
3 cups sugar
2 tablespoons lemon juice

Preheat oven to 350°F.

To prepare Pastry: Combine nuts, sugar, cinnamon, cloves, and nutmeg. Set aside.

Brush an 11x16-inch baking pan with butter. Place a sheet of the phyllo pastry in buttered pan; brush pastry with butter. Repeat until there are four pastry sheets in the pan, making sure to brush each sheet with butter. Sprinkle some of the nut mixture over pastry sheets.

Repeat the above steps with three pastry sheets, brushing each with butter. Top with some of the nut mixture. Continue alternating layers, ending with four layers of butter-brushed pastry sheets. Brush top layer with butter. Using a sharp knife or razor blade, cut the top layer of pastry sheets into diamond shapes. Do not cut all the way through all layers. Bake at 350°F for 1 hour or until lightly browned.

To prepare Syrup: Combine water, sugar, and lemon juice in a saucepan. Simmer over low heat until mixture thickens slightly (50 to 60 minutes). Cool syrup completely. Pour syrup over warm pastry. When pastry is cool, cut through scored diamond shapes.

Yield: 25 to 30 pieces

Tiropetes
(Cheese Triangles)

1 pound feta cheese, crumbled
³/₄ cup cottage cheese
3 eggs, beaten

Dash of pepper
1 pound phyllo pastry sheets, thawed
¹/₂ pound (2 sticks) butter, melted

Preheat oven to 350°F.

In a mixing bowl, combine feta cheese, cottage cheese, eggs, and pepper; mix thoroughly. Cut each phyllo pastry sheet lengthwise into five strips. Working with one strip at a time, brush pastry with butter. Place a rounded teaspoonful of the cheese mixture near one end of the strip. Fold end of strip over cheese mixture to form a triangle, and continue folding pastry over filling to form a triangle-shaped packet. (See note below.) Repeat this procedure until all pastry strips and cheese filling are used.

Place cheese triangles on an ungreased baking sheet. Bake at 350°F for 20 minutes or until golden brown. Serve warm or cooled.

Yield: 30 to 45 triangles

Note: These multilayered cheese pastries freeze beautifully, before or after baking. The secret to their triangle shape is folding the pastry strips as if you were folding a flag.

Pastitsio
(Macaroni and Meat Casserole)

1 package (16 ounces) macaroni
1/2 pound (2 sticks) butter, divided
1 large onion, finely chopped
1 pound ground beef
1 can (8 ounces) tomato sauce
Salt and pepper to taste
Dash of cinnamon

1/2 cup flour
3 cups milk
1/2 teaspoon salt
9 eggs
1 can (6 to 8 ounces) grated Romano
  cheese

Cook macaroni in boiling salted water until barely tender. Do not overcook. Rinse in cold water and drain thoroughly.

To prepare meat sauce, melt 1 stick butter in a large skillet. Add onion and sauté until golden brown. Add ground beef and cook until meat is browned and crumbly. Add tomato sauce, salt, pepper, and cinnamon; cover and simmer until mixture thickens slightly.

To prepare custard sauce, melt remaining 1 stick butter in a saucepan. Add flour, blending well. Gradually add milk and cook, stirring constantly, until mixture thickens. Add 1/2 teaspoon salt. Break eggs into a large mixing bowl and beat well. Add some of the hot mixture to the eggs and stir to blend well. Then slowly add remaining sauce to eggs, stirring until mixture thickens.

In a 9x13-inch baking pan, using half of the ingredients for each layer, alternate layers of macaroni, meat sauce, and Romano cheese. Repeat layers, reserving some cheese for garnish. Pour custard sauce evenly over layered ingredients and top with a sprinkling of Romano cheese. Bake at 350°F for 45 minutes or until golden brown.

Yield: 10 to 15 servings

Once every September the I.M.A. grounds
are enlivened with music, entertainment,
colorful displays, exhibits of arts and
crafts and thousands of people
marking Penrod Day, one of the
most exciting, cultural and
artistic happenings in the state.
The event is sponsored by the
Penrod Society of Indianapolis.

Afternoon at Oldfields

Banwari Prakash Singh

Penrod Arts Fair

Stop by the Indianapolis Museum of Art on the first Saturday after Labor Day, and you'll find a vivid splash of cultural experiences at the Penrod Arts Fair. For seven fun-filled hours, you can view the works of more than 250 artists and galleries, experience more than 25 entertainment offerings, enjoy specialties from more than 20 restaurants, and explore the displays of more than 60 cultural organizations. Called "Indiana's Nicest Day," Penrod has lived up to its billing since its inception in 1967. Here is the recipe for a Penrod specialty.

Peppercorn Salami Sandwich

1 roll (8 to 9 pounds) cotto sausage (see note below)
Mixture of yellow mustard and Grey Poupon mustard (to taste)
Kaiser rolls, split

Prepare a grill (preferably charcoal rather than gas) and heat coals until temperature is quite hot (about 30 to 45 minutes). Wrap sausage in double layers of aluminum foil and place on grill. Do not place directly over coals. Cover grill and cook for 45 minutes to 1 hour. When sausage is thoroughly heated, remove from grill and cut into thick slices. Heat Kaiser rolls on grill. Place slices of sausage on warm rolls and spread with mustard to taste.

Yield: 15 to 16 sandwiches

Note: Cotto sausage is a soft Italian salami with whole peppercorns.

Fiesta

Fiesta is a celebration of Indianapolis' Hispanic heritage. The one-day festival is held the third Saturday in September on the American Legion Mall and Veterans Memorial Plaza. Fiesta is a family event with live Latin music, dancing, and authentic Latin and American food. It also features Latin arts and crafts, as well as educational and cultural exhibits. A fixture on the downtown festival scene since 1981, Fiesta draws thousands of visitors each year.

Gazpacho
(Cold Fresh Vegetable Soup)

4 cups water
3 tablespoons vegetable oil
2 tablespoons red-wine vinegar
1 clove garlic, crushed
1/2 teaspoon salt
1/4 teaspoon black pepper
4 tomatoes, diced

2 cucumbers, diced
2 onions, diced
2 sweet green peppers, diced
Coarse bread crumbs or bread cubes,
    chopped onions, or grated Parmesan
    cheese (for garnish)

In a mixing bowl, combine water, oil, vinegar, garlic, salt, and black pepper. Set aside while preparing the vegetables. In a large bowl, combine tomatoes, cucumbers, onions, and green peppers. Strain liquid and discard garlic pulp. Add seasoned liquid to vegetables and stir to mix well. Cover and refrigerate for several hours. Garnish with desired topping before serving.

Yield: 6 servings

Fricasé de Pollo
(Chicken Fricassee)

1 chicken (about 3 pounds)
2 cloves garlic, chopped
2 tablespoons vinegar
1 bay leaf
1 tablespoon salt
$^1/_2$ teaspoon oregano
$^1/_4$ teaspoon black pepper
3 cups water
3 medium potatoes, cubed

2 sweet red peppers, sliced
1 small onion, sliced
$^3/_4$ cup cubed ham (about $^1/_4$ pound)
$^1/_2$ cup black olives, chopped
$^1/_2$ cup tomato sauce
$^1/_2$ cup vegetable oil
1 tablespoon capers
1 can (16 ounces) peas, drained (optional)

Clean chicken and cut into serving pieces. In a large bowl, combine garlic, vinegar, bay leaf, salt, oregano, and black pepper; mix well. Add chicken to bowl, turning to coat all sides with seasonings. Cover and refrigerate for 2 to 3 hours.

Place chicken in a deep cooking pot or Dutch oven. Add water, potatoes, peppers, onion, ham, olives, tomato sauce, vegetable oil, and capers; bring to a boil. Stir gently to mix; cover and reduce heat. Simmer about 30 minutes or until chicken and potatoes are tender. Add peas and simmer, uncovered, about 15 minutes longer.

Yield: 6 to 8 servings

Flan
(Caramel Custard)

1 cup sugar, divided
3 tablespoons boiling water
3 cups milk

1 cinnamon stick
4 eggs

Preheat oven to 325°F.

Place ³/₄ cup sugar in a heavy skillet over medium-high heat; cook, stirring constantly, until sugar melts and is a caramel color. Add boiling water very slowly, stirring quickly. Pour mixture into a 1-quart casserole. Tilt and turn the casserole so sugar mixture coats bottom and sides of dish. Set aside.

In a saucepan, combine remaining ¹/₄ cup sugar, milk, and cinnamon stick. Heat slowly just to the boiling point, but do not boil. Remove cinnamon stick. Break eggs into a mixing bowl and beat slightly. Slowly add milk mixture to eggs, stirring until well blended. Strain mixture and pour into sugar-coated casserole. Place casserole in a larger pan and pour hot water into pan to a depth of one inch. Bake at 325°F for 55 to 60 minutes or until a knife inserted in the center of the custard comes out clean. Remove from oven and cool. Refrigerate until thoroughly chilled. Loosen edges of custard and unmold onto a serving plate. Let sit a few minutes before serving so sauce will run down the sides of the flan.

Yield: 5 or 6 servings

Western Festival

The Western Festival is held the third Saturday in September at the Eiteljorg Museum of American Indians and Western Art, which displays both Native American art and Western paintings and bronzes, including works by Frederic Remington and Charles M. Russell. This festival features the Some Like It Hot Chili Cookoff and the Hoosier Beef BBQ Showdown, both of which offer public tasting. Here are two winning recipes to sample at home.

BS Secret Beef Barbecue

¹/₃ cup paprika
2 tablespoons black pepper
2 tablespoons salt
2 tablespoons sugar
1 tablespoon chili powder

1 tablespoon garlic powder
1 tablespoon onion powder
1 teaspoon cayenne pepper
6 to 8 pounds beef brisket
Apple juice

Combine all seasonings in a small bowl and mix to blend. Coat brisket with seasoning mixture. Place brisket in a plastic bag, seal, and refrigerate 6 to 8 hours.

Remove brisket from refrigerator and bring to room temperature. Prepare charcoal grill for cooking. Place brisket fat side up on grill. Do not place directly over coals. Cook at 225–250°F for 60 to 75 minutes per pound, misting with apple juice once an hour. When cooked to desired doneness, remove meat from grill and let stand for 20 minutes. Cut meat against the grain and serve with LBJ's Favorite Barbecue Sauce.

Yield: 12 to 14 servings

LBJ's Favorite Barbecue Sauce

3 cups ketchup
1 cup honey
1 medium onion, finely chopped
1 sweet green pepper, finely chopped
$^1/_2$ cup firmly packed brown sugar

$^1/_2$ cup water
$^1/_2$ cup Worcestershire sauce
2 tablespoons Tabasco
2 teaspoons garlic powder

Combine all ingredients in a saucepan and bring to a boil. Reduce heat and simmer until onion and green pepper are tender.

Yield: about 5$^1/_2$ cups sauce

Chili Con Carter

2 pounds chuck roast, cut into $^1/_2$-inch
  cubes, or ground chuck
1 pound bulk hot Italian sausage
1 quart (4 cups) chicken broth
1 can (15 ounces) tomato sauce
4 cloves garlic, minced
3 medium onions, minced

3 mild banana peppers, minced
4 tablespoons ground mild chilies
3 tablespoons cumin
3 tablespoons brown sugar
2$^1/_2$ tablespoons paprika
$^1/_2$ teaspoon white pepper

Sauté cubed chuck roast and sausage in a large skillet or Dutch oven until browned; drain off any excess fat. Add all remaining ingredients and bring to a boil. Reduce heat and simmer 1 to 2 hours, stirring occasionally. Chili should be thick and smooth.

Yield: 6 to 8 servings

Applefest

First held in 1994, Applefest is quickly becoming an autumn tradition. Presented in October at Park Tudor School, the event features fun for the entire family—games, entertainment, arts and crafts, an eight-foot tall Talking Apple Tree that shares apple lore, riddles and stories, an apple baking contest, and a food frenzy of irresistible treats. Plus, the Lilly Orchard Store offers up apples, cider, candies, and jams. Here's a recipe from the festival that draws rave reviews.

Simple Apple Crisp

4 cups sliced apples
$^1/_3$ cup water
1 teaspoon cinnamon
$^1/_4$ teaspoon salt

1 cup sugar
$^3/_4$ cup flour
$^1/_3$ cup butter, softened
Ice cream (if desired)

Preheat oven to 350°F.

Place apples in an 8x8-inch baking dish. Sprinkle water, cinnamon, and salt over apples. In a mixing bowl, combine sugar, flour, and butter; mix with a fork until mixture resembles coarse crumbs. Sprinkle crumb mixture evenly over apples. Bake at 350°F for 40 to 45 minutes. Serve with a scoop of ice cream.

Yield: 4 to 6 servings

CIRCLE THEATRE - 1916
HOME OF THE INDIANAPOLIS SYMPHONY ORCHESTRA
RENAMED HILBERT CIRCLE THEATRE - 1996

International Festival

A celebration of cultures, the International Festival presents the very best of ethnic entertainment, foods, merchandise, and crafts. Each year, about 20,000 people visit the "villages" that represent the four regions of the world: Africa, the Americas, Asia, and Europe. Now a three-day event held in October, the first "official" International Festival was held in 1976. A visit to the International Festival helps everyone become more aware of Indiana's rich ethnic heritage.

Sukiyaki
(Japanese Glazed Pork Steaks)

$1/2$ teaspoon water
$1/4$ teaspoon dry mustard
$1/2$ cup soy sauce
3 cloves garlic, minced
2 tablespoons vegetable oil

1 tablespoon grated fresh ginger root
1 tablespoon sherry
1 tablespoon sugar
1 tablespoon vinegar
4 pork steaks, sliced thin

Mix water and dry mustard in a container with a cover. Add soy sauce, garlic, oil, ginger, sherry, sugar, and vinegar. Cover and let sit for 6 to 8 hours.

Place meat in a shallow dish or bowl; pour marinade over meat and let sit for 20 minutes. Drain marinade and discard. Sauté meat in a skillet until browned on both sides; reduce heat and cook 20 minutes longer.

Yield: 4 servings

Irish Colcannon

1¹/₂ pounds potatoes, peeled and
    cut into cubes
1¹/₂ cups finely chopped cabbage
1 tablespoon butter

1 tablespoon dried parsley flakes
1¹/₂ cups milk
6 scallions, chopped
Salt and pepper to taste

In separate pans, boil potatoes and cabbage until tender. Drain potatoes and mash. Drain cabbage and combine with butter and parsley. Heat milk just to the boiling point, but do not boil. Add hot milk and scallions to potatoes and beat until fluffy. Add cabbage to potatoes and mix well. Season with salt and pepper. Serve hot.

Yield: 6 to 8 servings

Note: This dish is served on All Saints' Eve (Halloween). Small trinkets, each of which has a meaning, are wrapped in white paper and hidden in the dish before it is served. The token you get in your serving tells your destiny for the coming year—a wedding ring means you will marry and live happily ever after; a coin signals wealth; a thimble or a button means you will not marry; a miniature horseshoe means good fortune.

Scottish Hot Pot

6 shoulder lamb chops, trimmed of
   excess fat
Salt and pepper to taste
2 large onions, sliced
$^{1}/_{2}$ pound fresh whole mushrooms

$2^{1}/_{2}$ cups beef broth
2 pounds new red potatoes, sliced
   (do not peel)
2 tablespoons butter, divided

Preheat oven to 350°F.

Place chops in a shallow casserole. Season with salt and pepper. Arrange onion slices on top of chops. Place mushrooms on top of onions. Add beef broth. Arrange potatoes over top, overlapping the slices. Dot with half of the butter, cut into small pieces. Cover and bake at 350°F for 1 hour. Remove cover and dot with remaining butter. Bake, uncovered, 45 minutes longer or until potatoes are done.

Yield: 6 servings

Chinese Sliced Beef with Broccoli

$1^1/_2$ pounds flank steak, trimmed
   of all fat
4 tablespoons cornstarch, divided
3 tablespoons soy sauce, divided
2 tablespoons pale dry sherry
2 tablespoons sugar, divided
1 tablespoon sesame oil
6 tablespoons cold water
1 bunch fresh broccoli

$^1/_2$ cup vegetable oil, divided
1 can (7 ounces) button mushrooms,
   drained
1 can (8 ounces) bamboo shoots or
   water chestnuts, drained
2 teaspoons salt
4 slices fresh ginger root, peeled and
   chopped
Hot cooked rice

Slice steak across the grain into 2x$^1/_2$-inch strips. In a mixing bowl, combine 2 tablespoons cornstarch, 1 tablespoon soy sauce, sherry, 1 tablespoon sugar, and sesame oil; mix well. Add strips of steak to mixture and stir to coat well. Cover and refrigerate for about 30 minutes. In a separate bowl, combine remaining 2 tablespoons cornstarch, 2 tablespoons soy sauce, 1 tablespoon sugar, and water; mix well. Set aside.

Trim broccoli and cut into 2-inch pieces. Heat 3 tablespoons oil in a wok or large skillet until very hot. Reduce heat to moderate temperature and stir-fry broccoli for 3 to 5 minutes. Add mushrooms, bamboo shoots or water chestnuts, and salt. Cook 5 minutes longer or until vegetables are heated through and broccoli is still crisp. Remove from pan and keep warm.

Add remaining oil to pan and heat until very hot. Add ginger root and stir-fry for a few seconds. Drain marinade from meat and discard. Add meat to skillet and stir-fry at high temperature for 5 to 7 minutes. Beef should be slightly rare. Add reserved seasoning sauce and cook until thick and bubbly. Add cooked vegetables and cook until thoroughly heated. Serve with hot cooked rice.

Yield: 6 to 8 servings

Indian Baked Chicken with Spices

$^1/_2$ cup vegetable oil
2 large onions, diced
4 whole cloves
2 cardamom seeds, split
1 cinnamon stick, 1 inch long
1 tablespoon finely chopped garlic
1 tablespoon grated fresh ginger root
1 large tomato, diced
2 tablespoons chopped fresh cilantro

1 tablespoon ground coriander
$^1/_2$ teaspoon ground turmeric
$^1/_4$ teaspoon ground red pepper
6 boneless, skinless chicken breasts
Salt to taste
1 cup dairy sour cream
$^1/_2$ cup plain yogurt
Diced tomatoes (for garnish)
Chopped cilantro (for garnish)

Heat oil in a 6-quart stainless frying pan. Add onions, cloves, cardamom seeds, cinnamon stick, garlic, and ginger; sauté until onions are transparent. Add tomato, cilantro, coriander, turmeric, and red pepper; sauté 1 minute. Add chicken and salt; cover and cook over medium-low heat about 20 minutes or until chicken breasts begin to look done.

Add sour cream and yogurt; stir to blend well. Cover and cook over medium-low heat 10 to 15 minutes longer. Transfer mixture to a shallow baking dish. Bake at 375°F for 1 hour. Garnish with tomatoes and cilantro before serving.

Yield: 6 servings

Philippine Chicken Wings

3 pounds chicken wings
$^1/_4$ cup vinegar
3 cloves garlic, mashed
1 tablespoon pickling spice

1 tablespoon soy sauce
Salt and pepper to taste
1 cup water
$^1/_2$ cup (1 stick) butter, melted

Cut off and discard tips of chicken wings. In a large bowl, combine vinegar, garlic, pickling spice, soy sauce, salt, and pepper; mix well. Add chicken wings and stir so all pieces are coated with marinade. Cover and refrigerate for 2 hours.

Place chicken wings and marinade in a saucepan; add water and bring to a boil. Simmer 10 minutes. Drain liquid and discard. Place chicken wings in a shallow roasting pan and drizzle with butter. Bake at 350°F for 15 to 20 minutes or until golden brown and tender.

Yield: 4 to 6 servings

Estonian Nut Crisps

1/2 cup (1 stick) butter
1 cup firmly packed brown sugar
1 large egg
1 teaspoon vanilla extract
1 cup flour

1/2 teaspoon salt
1/2 teaspoon baking soda
1/2 cup finely chopped pecans or walnuts
Granulated sugar (for garnish)

Grease a baking sheet. Preheat oven to 325°F.

In a mixing bowl, cream butter and brown sugar until fluffy. Add egg and vanilla and beat well. Combine flour, salt, and baking soda; blend into creamed mixture. Add nuts and mix well. Drop teaspoonfuls of batter two inches apart onto prepared baking sheet. Dampen the bottom of a small glass and dip into sugar; then use the glass to press a cookie quite thin. Repeat this process until all cookies have been pressed. Bake at 325°F for 8 minutes. Cookies will be light brown and crispy.

Yield: about 24 cookies

Festival of Gingerbread

The festival year in Indianapolis comes to a joyful close with Conner Prairie's Festival of Gingerbread, a holiday treat since 1989. Featuring more than 100 gingerbread creations made by children and adults, this is the largest exhibition of its kind in the Midwest. Conner Prairie, an Earlham College museum, is a living history museum focusing on life for Indiana settlers in the early 19th century. The following are original "receipts" (recipes) from the 1830s.

Gingerbread

1 cup sugar
$^{1}/_{2}$ cup (1 stick) butter
1 egg
1 cup molasses

1 cup soured milk (see note below)
1 teaspoon baking soda
3 cups flour
1 teaspoon ground ginger

Grease a 13x9-inch baking pan. Preheat oven to 350°F.

Combine sugar and butter in a mixing bowl. Add egg and beat well. Add molasses. Combine soured milk and soda; stir to mix. Add milk to creamed mixture and blend well. Add flour and ginger; mix well. Spread batter in prepared pan. Bake at 350°F for 30 to 40 minutes or until firm.

Yield: 8 to 10 servings

Note: To make soured milk, place 1 tablespoon lemon juice in a 1-cup glass measure. Add milk to fill the cup. Let sit for 5 minutes before using.

Hot Spiced Cider

1 teaspoon whole cloves
1 teaspoon ground nutmeg
1 quart (4 cups) apple cider

4 tablespoons lemon juice
3 cinnamon sticks

Tie cloves and nutmeg in a small cheesecloth bag; set aside. Combine cider, lemon juice, and cinnamon sticks in a pan (do not use an iron pan). Simmer cider mixture for 15 minutes. Add spice bag and simmer until desired flavor is attained.

Yield: 4 to 6 servings

Market Square Arena / City County Bldg.

Indianapolis Festivals Calendar

May
500 Festival, Throughout the month

June
Balkan Festival, First weekend
Italian Street Festival, Second weekend
Strawberry Festival, Second or third Thursday
Midsummer Fest, First Saturday following the summer solstice

July
Indiana Black Expo's Summer Celebration, Third week

September
Oktoberfest, First two weekends (or may begin in late August)
Greek Festival, First weekend after Labor Day
Penrod Arts Fair, First Saturday after Labor Day
Fiesta, Third Saturday
Western Festival, Third Saturday

October
Applefest, First Saturday
International Festival, Mid-month

December
Festival of Gingerbread, Throughout the month

For more information about these and other festivals in Indianapolis, contact:

Indianapolis Convention & Visitors Association
One RCA Dome, Suite 100
Indianapolis, IN 46225
Phone (317) 684-2450 or (800) 323-4639

Notes

Notes

Notes

Index